Dear
Yankee

Library of Congress Cataloging in Publications Data:

Farrow, Peter.
  Dear yankee.

  1. American wit and humor. I. Title.
PS3556.A7783D4   1985   816'.54   85-8091
  ISBN 0-89621-091-X (pbk.)

Dear Yankee

by
Peter Farrow

THORNDIKE PRESS • THORNDIKE, MAINE

FOREWORD

F ENCOUNTERS WITH YANKEES sometimes seem chilly, the trouble usually boils down to a matter of manners. Take, for example, the case of John Doe (not his real name) who, having lost his way, drove up into a rural New England dooryard, popped up to the house and knocked to ask directions. The only response was the sound of a bolt being slammed into place—and it didn't sound quite like a *door* bolt, either.

When he tried the next house, the door opened a crack. John smiled, said he was lost and asked if 427 would take him to 302. "Depends which way you're pointed," was all the answer he got.

Asking again, at a third house, if 427 would take him to 302, the Yankee-in-residence looked him over for a long minute, then burst out with, "Oh, Gawd! I hope so!"

Swearing he'd never ask another Yankee for anything, John roared off in a huff, never realizing that the fault wasn't with Yankees but with himself: he'd committed seven social blunders in six minutes—by no means a record, but enough to sct any Yankee's teeth on edge.

So it seemed that, along with those little books telling tourists how to dissect boiled lobsters, whittle trunnels, pronounce *"Ayuh"* and practice other native arts, there ought to be a guide to Yankee Manners. Nothing massive, understand; just enough to save strangers from the major social pitfalls.

Thus this book. It won't turn you into a Yankee, of course. But it may help take a little of the chill off.

Since you can't practice Yankee Manners unless you get here in the first place, we'll begin by answering poor John—even if he hasn't bothered to ask yet.

GETTING HERE

Dear John:

It wasn't so much what you did but the way you went at it.

FIRST, you don't drive right up into a Yankee's dooryard, blocking all hope of escape. You park your car at some distance short of near but in full view of the house. Let your engine idle to show your intentions are temporary, and step out into clear sight. *Stay* that way for ten minutes or so. All this gives the Yankee a chance to look you over, size you up, prise the cut of your jib and maybe come out under his own steam—or at least get comfortably into hiding.

SECOND, you don't just pop right up to his door. Saunter, stroll, amble, shuffle or trudge but don't *hurry*. You can squint at the sky but never at the surroundings, however amazing.

THIRD, knock just three well-spaced, sort of stately taps, that's all. More or faster is considered frantic if not outright rabid.

FOURTH, for pity's sake don't *smile*. What's there to smile about? Especially when you're saying you're lost—which you shouldn't, in the first place. *Lost* is a Biblical word, as in *lost tribe, lost lamb, lost soul.* Its secular use is reserved for the deeper reaches of the Atlantic, such as *lost at sea, lost with all hands,* though it might be stretched to cover babes under three deep in the Allagash. So instead say, "I seem to be *a mite turned around* . . ." indicating temporary confusion, not mortal perdition. After all, you're only asking to be helped, not saved.

FIFTH, don't ask for information, ask for *advice.* Instead of saying, "Will 427 get me to 302?" say, "Would you tell me *the best way* to get to Fustis Junction?"

SIXTH, don't rattle off a bunch of numbers! Numbers grate worse on the Yankee ear than a New Yorker's vowels. We're still a century shy of agreeing that Froley's Pike is now labelled 302 and the Old County Stage Road has been reduced to a fleeting iota of some rutless wonder dubbed 427.

Your SEVENTH blunder was swearing you'd never ask a Yankee anything again. The only thing that can pester a Yankee worse than being asked is *not* being asked. While we do admire Independence, being the inventors of that virtue, we mistrust its wanton use by others.

WALL-TO-WALL BASICS

Dear Yankee:

I've read all the best books on etiquette and tried everything they say, but nothing seems to work up here.

Bewildered

Dear Bewildered:

Etiquette is no substitute for manners. While a Yankee can point a pinky with the best, there is *no such thing* as Yankee etiquette. If you look it up, you'll see that *etiquette* comes from a French word for *ticket*—something you show at the door to get in. Most people figure if only they can pile up etiquettes enough, they can get in anywhere. That's where the trouble starts: Yankees don't want to get *in* anywhere. To us, *keeping out* is the main idea.

Dear Yankee:

Yankees seem to have a protective wall around them all the time! But didn't Robert Frost tell us that walls are wrong?

Just Checking

Dear Just Checking:

Frost was no Yankee, only a transplanted Californian who, rumor has it, never even mastered *"Ayuh"* after 90 years of trying. "Something there is that does not love a wall" perhaps, but it sure isn't a Yankee. A Yankee without a wall is about as comfortable as a shucked clam.

Dear Yankee:

How does one get through to you people?

Curious

Dear Curious:

Three ways, to start. First, stop looking for chinks to stick your etiquettes into; second, understand that those walls are just as much to keep the Yankee out of your affairs as to keep you out of his; and third, start laying up a few walls of your own.

PLEASE, THANK YOU, and OTHER BLUNDERS

Dear Yankee:

I don't care what your manners are! It seems to me you Yankees could at least say please and thank you once in a while!

Outraged

Dear Outraged:

To Yankees, both are confessions. *Please* confesses being in need; *thank you* admits being in debt. Yankee manners render both unnecessary. For example, instead of saying, "Please pass the salt," a Yankee will say, to no one in particular, "Might a person have some salt, d'you suppose?" Nothing could be more polite, but notice that no need is confessed, no plea made, and no demand imposed on anyone else.

The same for *thank you*. Instead of running off at the mouth for hours on end, we just give an abrupt little bob of the head, such as might be caused by driving over a bump in the road. In fact, bumps in the road are called *thank-you-marms*.

Dear Yankee:

Why are you Yankees so grim? I've smiled and smiled and smiled, but no one has ever smiled back.

Distraught

Dear Distraught:

We presume that there must be something to smile *about*. So don't feel distraught, feel grateful. For if a Yankee does smile, it may mean he's found something funny about *you*. He probably has, but his good manners forbid his showing it. That eternal grimness around the Yankee mouth, by the way, comes from years of holding in snickers.

Still, to be truly smiled on by a Yankee can be one of Life's crowning experiences. I know. It's happened to me nearly twice.

DROPPING IN, CALLING
and RELATED DISASTERS

Dear Yankee:

For pity's sake, isn't it possible to just drop in and pay a friendly call now and then? Sign me,

Rebuffed

Dear Rebuffed:

Excepting sheriffs, game wardens and IRS agents, nobody drops *in* on a Yankee. All others drop *by*. A good half of Yankee manners is just mastering the prepositions: *In* is an act of penetration; *by* but a glancing blow. It works to your advantage, too, for dropping *by* implies that you're actually on your way to somewhere else. That not only gives the Yankee hope of brevity, but gives you an excuse to get away.

And don't call it a *call*. *Call* refers to business or mere duty—and again, watch those prepositions: One calls *at* the bank, the courthouse, the butcher; one calls *on* parsons, widows and the deserving poor.

Dear Yankee:

I dropped by a neighbor's house and his wife kept me standing on the doorstep in a pouring rain for an hour till he came up from the barn. It wasn't that she was unfriendly, but she just wouldn't budge an inch to let me in.

Drenched to the Marrow

Dear Drenched:

You shouldn't even have *thought* about getting inside—not even if she'd offered. A man never enters a house unless and until the man-of-the-house is actually present. It's not that Yankees distrust their wives; it's just that they know their neighbors' habits. Nothing cooks up a pot of gossip quicker, even if the missus is 96 years old and you're on the doorstep with two broken legs.

TAPROOM TIPS

Dear Yankee:

I went into a bar hoping to take a little of the chill off my bones, but I wound up chillier than I began. What did I do wrong?

Frigid

Dear Frigid:

Plenty, probably. But your likeliest blunder was picking the wrong place to begin with. While establishments for wayside refreshment go by many names—bar, tavern, taproom, pub, lounge and the like—at heart there are only two kinds, *public* and *local,* and you'd be wise to learn to tell them apart. Any place that proclaims Cocktails, Happy Hours and is swathed in Muzak, can be considered public and therefore safe. But if it leans more to juke than Muzak and proclaims itself by the number of pickup trucks parked outside— well that, Mister Man, is a local and it's best passed by.

. . . But what if the only place is a local?

Enter invisibly, drink modestly, depart silently—
and soon.

. . . Why did the bartender look so queer when
I asked for a Pink Squirrel?

Don't expect to meet Pink Squirrels, Daiquiris, Tia
Marias or Misty Ladies (whatever they are) at the local
bar. Mint gin is about as fancy as it gets, and most beer
is imported from no farther away than Milwaukee
which, for Yankees, is far enough.
However, this doesn't mean that there's not a definite
delicacy to Yankee tippling. Drinks are neither gulped,
sipped nor tossed down. They are— there's no other
word for it—*imbibed:* sort of surrounded and silently
absorbed, like a starfish operating on a clam. In fact,
I've never seen a Yankee actually *drink*. Even with beer,
two swallows in a row is considered gluttony, and in all
cases, it's the glass, not the head, that's tipped.

. . . My girlfriend was with me, and she got
even chillier than I did . . .

She was visible, that's why. You might remind her
gently that while females may stand at the bar, and
women sit at the bar, *ladies* take their pleasures in a
booth. Some places even have a Ladies Entrance around
in back. In any event, a local is no place to start an ERA
drive, at least not in a milltown on Friday night.

BOATING

Dear Yankee:

Your manners must end at high-water mark! It seems to me the ocean should be big enough for both of us to go boating!

Irate

Dear Irate:

Our Yankee manners don't end at high-water mark, just our charity towards blunders. And *both* of us can't "go boating," anyway. Yankees go fishing, dragging, seining, clamming, lobstering, and we use boats to do it, but we're *working,* not boating. That's strictly for Tourists, Summer Complaints and other strangers, whose first rule should be: Steer wide of working boats. Those craft are our tools, and the ocean's our workplace.

Dear Yankee:

I was nearly run down by a lobsterboat today! Don't you Yankees know that the rules of the road require power to give way to sail?

Close Call

Dear Close:

By gosh, you're right! Next time, you just stop the feller and tell him all about that.

Dear Yankee:

When I go out deep-sea fishing, I get—well, spattered. Do even the gulls hate me?

Bombarded

Dear Bombarded:

Chances are you've been tailing commercial party boats out, since their skippers know where the big ones really are, figuring you can get in on it without paying. So the chances are, too, that the skipper ahead is just gently reminding you that this is poor manners by chumming a little bait behind him. Gulls tend to lighten load before they feed.

Dear Yankee:

The neck of our little harbor is so clotted up with lobsterpot buoys you can hardly see the water between them, yet the lobstermen get ferocious if I so much as nudge one. Why can't they be set somewhere else? They're hazards to navigation!

Deeply Annoyed

Dear Deeply:

That would be a hazard to lobstering. Instead, look on them as a challenge to your steermanship, like a slalom course—even if rumor does have it that nine out of ten of those buoys are there just for the natives' amusement, with naught but rocks on their nether ends.

Dear Yankee:

My wife asked me to get her a couple of those buoys to take home for conversation pieces. Would anyone mind if I took them? There'd still be that little bottle thing to show where the lobsterpot was, after all.

Collector

Dear Collector:

Now you go right ahead and do that. You pay out good money up here and you're entitled to a little souvenir or two. Of course, the old Yankee rule is: First shot at the waterline; second, below it; third, through the meddler. However, we've simplified things now: we've eliminated the first two shots.

Dear Yankee:

. . . With all these rules and manners you've got about boating, I feel just plain frustrated!

Puckered

Dear Puckered:

Then why don't you do like we do? Go toot at a draw-bridge and watch the cars pile up. It's a great soother!

VISITING

Dear Yankee:

We've been coming up here every summer for twenty years, but we're never invited anywhere! I don't care what you say: I think you Yankees are just plain inhospitable!

Ruffled

Dear Ruffled:

Now granted, a Yankee may not flag you down in mid-turnpike to yell, "Howdy, y'all! Ah'm Beauregard Bunbottom and Ah'm hospitable as all git out!" like they do down South. But Yankee hospitality is of a far higher order. In fact, the very thing that's ruffling your feathers is really the highest kind of Yankee manners. We hold to the old copybook maxim:

> "A favor bestowed
> Is a favor owed . . ."

So by *not* inviting you, they're not only saving themselves bother but keeping you out of social debt, than which there is nothing more wretched.

. . . But can't one just visit a Yankee?

Visiting is taken seriously, for a visit is a delicate thing to define. "Whether a visit shall seem a visitation," old Noah Webster put it, "Depends a good deal on the visitor . . ." It might be useful to remember that Noah, a born-in-the-bosom Yankee, was an authority on pestilences as well as dictionaries. So rather than risk seeming like some vengeance of a wrathful god, Yankees just don't visit much at all, not even with each other. Visit if you must, but remember that nowhere else may you be more naked to the winds of blunder.

Dear Yankee:

When I go visiting, which door should I knock on—the front or the back?

Confused

Dear Confused:

Now that is truly a delicate matter indeed, for choosing doors is really a self-appraisal of your standing in the family's affections. In the old days, the front door was used only for parsons and funerals, leading as it did directly to the parlor. Today, of course, the parlor has eroded to a mere livingroom. But the actual Yankee *living* room—the true heart of the household—is the kitchen, as it's always been. However, the kitchen door is in the back, so some feel insulted at the thought of "going around to the back," even though Yankee houses have *no* back door, in the social sense. It's just called *the door,* while the front one is *the best door.* So the question really is: Do you feel yourself worthy of the best door? Or, on the other hand, so intimate that you'd strike at the very heart of the family, the kitchen?

So rather than play Lady-or-Tiger, just don't knock on either. Putter around outside and wait to see which door *they* open; if it's the kitchen door, then you have truly Arrived.

Dear Yankee:

How long should a visit be?

Tentative

Dear Tentative:

Another delicate matter! You can begin to see by now why Yankees don't visit much. A visit, since you asked, should not be so short as to seem a call or duty, nor so long as to seem familiar. Consulting your watch is deemed poor manners (as it should be everywhere), as no Yankee will be ruled by cogs and springs, let alone silicon chips. The best thing to consult is your host's thumbs. Pressed together, they merely signal decent attention. When press turns to twaddle, you should start making leaving noises. When twaddle turns to twiddle outright, bring your hat up to half-mast. If your host shifts upward in his chair, stand up before he does. This means you've called an end to things. If he stands first, it's a dismissal.

Dear Yankee:

Are there any certain signs that one is wearing out one's welcome?

Social Caller

Dear Social:

Keep an ear on the kitchen. The clatter of an impending meal's preparation is a signal not to be ignored. It expresses not only a hint but general opinion as well. Bear in mind that the Yankee housewife *can* prepare a meal for forty without the clink of a single potlid.

CONVERSATION

Dear Yankee:

I'm never quite sure what to talk about with you Yankees, because you all seem to say so little.

Loquacious

Dear Loquacious:

Yup.

Dear Yankee:

Do Yankees gossip?

Intrigued

Dear Intrigued:

Yankees *invented* gossip, and nowhere are tongues more finely honed than here. But after three hundred years of trying to keep the blood pure, by now most of us are related. This puts no crimp in *our* proceedings, understand, but others should remember that blood runs thicker than water before they attempt to join in.

Dear Yankee:

I've always heard that Yankees are just full of salty tales and earthy epithets, but I haven't heard a single one yet.

Curious

Dear Curious:

Oh, we're full of 'em, all right. But the best ones are about tourists, From-Awayers and other strangers like you, so we just mind our manners and save them up till after Labor Day.

Dear Yankee:

We're rock-ribbed Republicans. Surely, then, politics at least is a safe subject up here?

Foursquare

Dear Foursquare:

It used to be, back when being a Democrat was looked upon as a temporary affliction, like wild oats, which most Yankees got over long before voting age. But lately, we've been finding a Democrat or two in every barrel. It's getting riskier by the minute. Besides, sometimes we Yankees like to pretend to be Democrats just to watch you get puckered. Steer clear of the whole mess.

Dear Yankee:

Why did things get so silent when I cheered the Red Sox?

Sports Fan

Dear Sport:

People from Boston, including ballplayers, are not Yankees, only Bostonians. Try cheering Milwaukee.

Dear Yankee:

I'm just wild about genealogy, and I'm trying to trace my family tree up here. But I don't get much help. What's wrong?

Trueblood

Dear Trueblood:

They may get the impression you're trying to worm your way into some local family inheritance. But more likely they're just plain bored. Nowadays, with every old freebooter and slaver sanitized into a Clipper Captain, horsethieves transformed into churchfounders and every bastard the true son of the Lost Dauphin, genealogy has become gawdawful dull. True Yankees didn't come over on the *Mayflower,* by the way. We were already here.

Dear Yankee:

Why is it you Yankees will talk about mosquitoes, but never mention black flies?

Bitten

27

Dear Bitten:
What black flies?

Dear Yankee:
With all these taboo subjects, then what on earth does one talk about?

Friendly

Dear Friendly:
What do you think God made weather for? Since no mortal can be blamed for it, and since there's always more than enough to go around, weather is a sure-fire hit for every time or occasion. Best of all, it stretches. Besides Weather at Present and Weather in General, there's Weather, This Year Compared to Last; Famous Weathers—Floods, Droughts, Blizzards and Outright Christers; there are Spells of Weather—Dry, Wet, Cold, Hot and Foggy. After Latest Springs and Earliest Freezes, you can move on to Bunions versus Official Forecasts; Signs of Weather including but by no means limited to Mackerels and Marestails, Weather Breeders, Goose-Thaws, March Fools and Fat Churchyards, which can bring the talk around to Sou'Westers, Nor'Easters, Spankers, Smackers and Catspaws. Not to mention some 27 distinct species of mud.

And if you run out of weather to talk about, likely you've run out of welcome, too. If not, then just plain silence is not to be despised. As the old copybook saith:

"Mouths maketh strangers,
Ears maketh friends . . ."

AT TABLE

Dear Yankee:

We were invited to dinner but when we arrived our hosts had already eaten and were getting ready for bed. What did we do wrong?

Disconcerted

Dear Disconcerted:

You arrived six hours late, that's all. The Yankee *dinner* is at noon; the evening meal is *supper,* and *lunch* is something carried in a *dinner-pail* to work or school. Breakfast is still in the morning, but don't expect it the minute you get up. All you may find is what used to be called a *rising* or *squib*—a slab of something set out the night before to see the Old Man through the chores, breakfast *never* being served till they're done.

Dear Yankee:

When we had supper with our Yankee neighbors, the man's wife simply wouldn't sit down with all the rest of us. Did we do something to offend her?

Eager to Please

Dear Eager:

Daow. That's only normal. Never be surprised if the Missus doesn't join the table but instead trots to serve everyone else. The Yankee prides himself on getting by without servants—which is why he marries.

. . . There was no spoon at my place setting. I made do somehow, though I did have a terrible time with the Jello . . .

Spoons and spoons aplenty were there all the time, staring you right in the eye. Yankees are famous spooners, and there being no way to predict who'll need how many, when or for what, oftentimes spoons are put all together in a *spoon-bowl* set in midtable. Help yourself as often as you please.

Forks, however, are a different matter. There's often only one apiece. Show no amazement, then, at the cry, "Save back your forks! We got pie coming!"

And while we're at it, we may as well mention that *saucers* are still sometimes used as God intended: to cool the contents of the cup, a mite being poured thereinto, blown thereupon and swerped therefrom. Don't try this yourself without practice, and make sure no one's sitting opposite you when you do.

Dear Yankee:

I've been taught to always leave a little on my plate "for Mr. Manners." But no one else seems to here.

Abstemious

Dear Abstemious:

Your problem boils down to a matter of biscuits. They're useful as well as edible, you know. Break, wrench or pry a cold one in two. The top half, called the *pusher,* is used throughout the meal for stopping any skittish morsel dead in its tracks so your fork can get a proper purchase. The bottom half, called the *sopper,* is later set innards-side-down on your plate, skewered with your fork and used to mop the plate clean. It's Yankee manners to literally polish off a meal. Including both pusher and sopper.

Dear Yankee:

Our neighbors are actual fishermen, hipboots and all, but they never serve any of their catch. Why?

Mystified

Dear Mystified:

Fish, like prophets, lack honor in their native land, and familiarity has bred contempt. So don't be surprised if the haddock comes bonelessly frozen from Boston or the tuna from Bumblebee. A few Yankees, victims of their own propaganda probably, do actually serve lobsters. While a colorful centerpiece, lobsters— long known as *mudroaches* or *spiders* and considered food fit only for chickens and the indigent —are not traditional Yankee fare. Neither is tuna, once called *horse-mackerel* and shot on sight, while mussels, as every Yankee knows, are pizen-pure and so left for gulls, crows and stray furriners.

STAYING ON

Dear Yankee:

We are not tourists! We bit the bullet and moved here, lock, stock and barrel. Yet everyone treats us as if we were summer complaints!

Mr. & Mrs. Newcome

Dear Newcomes:

There's *winter* complaints, too, you know.

Some say that Yankees look on tourists pretty much like the Indians looked on the first Yankees: unsightly, but they do stir up some trade. Of course, this isn't really so. But when, every year, more and more From-Awayers come up here and forget to leave, it can set a Yankee to remembering what *happened* to the Indians. So if you're *staying on,* as it's called, mind your Yankee Manners even closer—and master a few more, too. You're playing for keeps, after all.

Dear Yankee:

We put up a temporary roadside sign so friends could find us. They never did. Somehow it got blown down the road a mile. We think this was poor manners.

Irate

Dear Irate:

Having our roads and everything else numbered on us is bad enough, but being reminded that we're *out*-numbered is a breach of manners not quickly staunched. Next time, stand out by the road and wait for your friends. You probably won't be more unsightly. And, while we're at it, there are also those permanent, usually "rustic" signs we find nailed to some blameless tree. If they merely said "The Smiths," "The Jones," "The Pugburtles" and the like, they might be squeezed within the pale of propriety: after all, they *do* point to taxable property. But "Bide-A-We," "Pine-E-Vu," "Just Us Nine" maketh the Yankee gorge to rise. How would *you* feel if *your* grandfather's old West Forty was now called "Cooky's Nook"?

Dear Yankee:

We never trespass on our neighbors' land, but they go anywhere they please over ours, so we've been thinking of putting up no tresspassing signs.

Possessive

Dear Possessive:

Such signs aren't blunders, they're outright ruptures of Yankee manners. And if those signs also say NO HUNTING then, Mister Man, you've thrown down the gauntlet. You won't be met by Yankee wrath, understand. That we save up for minor matters like wars. What you'll face is sheer Yankee ingenuity. Yankees can trespass in ways I'm not traitor enough to divulge. And calling in the sheriff may not be helpful, either. He and the judge are probably deerhunters, too—and more than likely related.

. . . BUT DON'T ANY OF YOU YANKEES
HEED SIGNS?

Oh, indeed we do! For instance, I can name you
any number of volunteer firemen who wouldn't *think*
of going up some road marked PRIVATE!
KEEP OUT!

DEAR YANKEE:
WHY DOES EVERYBODY TURN GRIM
WHENEVER I MENTION MY PLACE?

HERE TO STAY

Dear Here:
Place is a word not dripped lightly from the Yankee
lip. You can buy a house, cottage, camp, farm, even a
mansion, but no one, not even a Yankee, can buy a
place. Place denotes a spot in God's scheme of things,
preordained not later than the Sixth Day of Creation.
It is coupled only with the original settler's name,
such as the Fustis Place, even though the final Fustis
died in 1760. So don't be vexed if you're known,
forever, only as "That feller who's staying on up to
the Fustis Place."

HUNTING

Dear Yankee:

In late October all the menfolk around here started acting terribly peculiar. What's up?

Perplexed

Dear Perplexed:

They're acting normal. It's the rest of the year that's peculiar. Every November first, the Yankee grows three inches taller, widens his shoulders by a foot; his eyes take on a primal glint, legs get lopey and feet fall like feathers. It is then, if ever, that Yankee smiles on Yankee, for come November the world is right again, Life's back to basics: the law's off deer.

Dear Yankee:

I understand that the first day of the season is for resident hunters only. I've been living here seven whole months now. Do I qualify?

Eager

Dear Eager:

The word *resident* should not be construed too closely for the first twenty years or so. Of course, you're welcome to try. Wear lots of orange.

Dear Yankee:

I brought down a twelve point buck with a single shot at 300 yards. It was the biggest and first deer tagged in the whole town. Not a soul congratulated me. Are Yankees poor sports?

Straight Shooter

Dear Straight:

No. We're not *sports* at all. Like *boating,* hunting is a serious matter. We don't stuff what we shoot; we eat it. What you should have done was complain about how tough and ronky the meat was bound to be.

Dear Yankee:

Don't you hunters realize that, in terms of cost, venison works out to well over twenty dollars a pound?

CPA

Dear CPA:

That may hold true for venison, whatever that is, but not for deermeat. At least, if it does, nobody ever mentions it.

Dear Yankee:

I don't hunt, and I see no reason why I should have to get all decked out in day-glo orange just to go to my mailbox!

Greenpeacer

Dear Greenpeacer:

Then dress any way you please. But remember that anything that's non-fluorescent and moves is considered edible until shot.

TOWN MEETING

Dear Yankee:

We've always been terribly civic-minded and we have some wonderful ideas for improving our little town. What are the proper manners for speaking up at town meeting?

Eager

Dear Eager:

For newcomers, there's only one rule about speaking up at town meeting: Don't.*

---

*For the first twenty-odd years, there may be two occasions when this mannerly silence may be broken. One is when you want an item on the warrant defeated. Then speak up loud and clear in favor. The other time is when you want an item passed. Oppose it.

HIRING

Dear Yankee:

We offer excellent wages for easy work, but we just can't seem to find anyone to hire.

Vexed

Dear Vexed:

If ever you want to see a Yankee turn into a block of solid granite, go wave some dollars in his face and tell him you want to hire him. A Yankee can be begged, borrowed, stolen or even married, but he is never for *hire*. Yankees work and work hard; they just don't work *for* anybody. One Yankee I know has been punching a clock at a shipyard for twenty-eight years, but what he's been doing all that time is "helping out over to the Yard . . ." A Yankee has to feel not just useful but helpful.

. . . Then how do we go about getting help?

You drop by, wrestle the weather for a spell, make leaving noises. Then and only then is the matter broached: "Oh, by the way, I've been meaning to ask you. Who might a feller get to help put up a house?" While he's pondering on that, you add, just a little wistfully, "Of course, I was hoping you weren't too busy yourself . . ."

It's no way guaranteed, but this *may* lead to his saying, "I dunno. What you got in mind?"

Dear Yankee:
Are Yankees expensive?

Pennywise

Dear Pennywise:
Never ask how much per hour. Instead, ask, "Oh, by the way: what d'you suppose might be enough for a job like that?"

Nor do you ever ask when he can start. Instead: "About how long d'you suppose a thing like that might take?" You can then plan your life accordingly, give or take a year or two. Whatever you do, don't stick around too close when he's working. Just keep within earshot, in case he needs you—to help out.

BORROWING

Dear Yankee:
Is it all right to borrow?

Tremulous

Dear Trem:
According to tradition, to hear the experts tell it, just the mere thought of borrowing borders on bad manners. Don't you believe it. This isn't true and never has been. Yankees borrow whether they need to or not, and it's as finely honed a social gambit as courting or politics. But before you get involved, you'd better realize that there are two kinds of borrowing. There's borrowing, and then there's *borrowing.* The words are exactly the same, but the first means with the owner's permission and knowledge aforehand. The second is without it. It's akin to *taking,* and you'd be wise to rack up about five generations here before you try. So we'll confine this to just borrowing.

It's not gone at directly, of course. The first rule is to never even hint that you need anything. However desperate you may be, you don't say, for instance, "Would you please lend me your hammer?" Instead, you ask for the *use* of it. That's critical, for that way nothing is borrowed at all, since it's the *borrower himself* who's going to supply the use. Borrowing is just as much a matter of strategy as it is of manners.

Dear Yankee:
I borrowed an axe and returned it the same day—and in far better shape than I got it. But my neighbor didn't seem too pleased: He's hardly spoken to me since.

Frosted

Dear Frosted:

You made two bad blunders there. First, you didn't borrow it long enough: You never gave him time enough to figure out what he could borrow in turn from you. This sort of ruined the whole game, like throwing in the towel during the first round. Second, he probably took your shining it all up and sharpening it as a reflection on his tool-keeping. But he'll probably get over it. Just give him a year or two then try again.

Dear Yankee:

What if a Yankee wants to borrow something from me?

Uncertain

Dear Uncertain:

That may be a sign you're being accepted. The rule is, never be eager to lend. Just ready to. Never say, "Why, sure! Glad to!" but deftly shift the focus from the item to the conditions of the loan: "Nails? Why I guess so. How long'll you be needing 'em?"

Dear Yankee:

I lost a hammer I borrowed, so I offered the man five times over what it was worth. He took the money, all right, but he didn't seem too pleased with me.

Mislaid

Dear Mislaid:

More blunders! You didn't *lose* it; you just seemed to have *misplaced* it. Anything misplaced should be *replaced*. Money just won't do it: not even a hundred dollar bill will drive a single nail.

Dear Yankee:

I loaned my neighbor a shovel and he still hasn't returned it. It's been over a year now. How do I get it back?

Snowbound

Dear Snowbound:

After a year, some Yankees may hold that a thing's not loaned, it's abandoned. But if you must try, never ask outright for its return. Instead, ask to *borrow it back* for a spell. If he's willing to *lend it back,* as it's called, take it and then just don't return it. After a year, you can consider it abandoned, too.

But if he's not willing to lend it back, then borrow something from him that's worth at least twice as much as your missing item—and sort of hold it hostage.

FINDING OUT

Dear Yankee:

I always heard about how helpful you Yankees are. But whenever I get into a jam of some kind, you turn your backs square on me every time.

Disconcerted

Dear Disconcerted:

You've just got to learn to distinguish between true distress and a mess. When a Yankee turns his back to you, he's just showing his good manners, the same as he would to a lady caught stark naked. A Yankee gets embarrassed real easy, even if you (or the lady) may not be.

Generally, backturning signifies that the Yankee knows something which you, obviously, *don't* know, but which anyone short of a total idjit should, could, must have realized beforehand without actually having to *find out*.

To save embarrassment, if not to you then at least to your Yankee neighbors, here's a partial list of some common back-turners. They're not blunders, exactly. Just blushers.

Mooring a boat in a cove that empties at low tide.

*

Wearing foul-weather gear on dry land.

*

Tapping oak trees for maple syrup.

*

Depending on city newspapers for accurate local tidetables.

*

Thinking mosquitoes quit on Labor Day.

*

Expecting wholesale fish prices at the dock.

*

Burning over a patch of poison ivy.

*

Building a house with a flat roof.

*

Boasting that your woodpile will get you through the winter.

*

Ignoring cattails, bullfrogs and other signs of a boghole in a road because you've got a four-wheel drive.

Add to these, of course: Thinking that Yankee Manners aren't really worth learning in the first place.

AFTERWORD

As we said in the beginning, this little book won't turn everybody into a Yankee. But a few are bound to think so, and that brings up the whole subject of *blending*—trying to look, talk and act like a Yankee. You won't fool anybody but yourself.

Blending, understand, isn't bad manners so much as it's poor sportsmanship, like dressing up in the enemy's uniform behind enemy lines. As with any other people under siege, we Yankees figure we have the right to know who's who. So don't feel downhearted if you never do quite master Yankee Manners. Just keep on being your own ridiculous, queer-talking, strange-acting, unsightly looking self. That way, you'll present such a clear target that we'll feel we can bag you at any time. And so we may just leave you alone long enough to get to know you. Even like you.

In the meantime, keep on plugging and remember:
The first three hundred years are always the hardest.